Budget Cooking for One

Book Two

Budget Recipes for One – The Art of Cooking for Yourself

Penelope R Oates

DISCLAIMER

Table of Contents

Introduction

Anyone Can Cook – Well Almost Anyone...

Cooking from scratch is a skill that everyone should be able to master, even with todays culture of fast food and TV dinners. But sadly, there are a lot of people who have never really got the hang of it; mainly because there are so many easy alternatives. Now I'm not trying to tell you that it's all bad – not at all. The advance in convenience products has given us all choices and choices are always good.

However, even though my five sons have grown and left home and I live alone, I very rarely resort to pre-prepared food. I aim to cook at least one meal each day using fresh ingredients.

If you think that it is much quicker to feed one person using convenience foods, you are mistaken.

Give some of the simple recipes in this book a try and I can guarantee that you will not spend much more time in the kitchen than you would if you had prepared a frozen dinner in a traditional oven.

When I was young there were not many convenience choices; no microwave ovens, no ready meals and not many homes even had a freezer. So my generation had no alternative but to learn to cook their meals from scratch, starting with fresh produce.

With hindsight, that was no bad thing because at least we knew for certain exactly what we were putting in our bodies, we knew exactly what was in our food.

Another benefit of yesteryear was, because there was no microwave to quickly reheat food, everyone was expected to sit down at the dinner table to eat a freshly prepared meal at the same time. Meals were almost a social occasion where the family could discuss their day and talk things over.

When my boys were growing up things were gradually changing. The microwave was the first thing I learned to embrace because it meant that if I had prepared a meal and one of them was delayed at a football match or a swimming event, I could reheat their meal quickly (or they could do it themselves...) without it drying out in the oven or me having to cook two separate meals.

The downside was 'family time' was diminishing somewhat. So I decided that we should have Sunday lunch together, this was non-negotiable! As they grew older it became a big event when they all began bringing girlfriends and later, wives, partners and children to Sunday lunch.

The other decision I had made early on in my boys lives was that they should all be able to cook.

Fortunately they all love cooking and now, 30+ years on, they can all cook good food from scratch. My eldest son's curries are legendary as are my youngest son's chicken dinners...

Now I wonder, in the 21st century, with all the knowledge that is available at our fingertips via the internet, including interesting recipes and cooking techniques from all over the world, why so many people don't cook using the fabulous fresh ingredients that are so readily available.

I also wonder if the unwillingness or inability to cook from fresh contributes massively to the Western world having so many weight related problems.

Top Tip:

Remember, if you are a beginner at cooking, YouTube is your friend. If there is a technique or recipe you read about that leaves you confused, go to YouTube and you will, almost certainly, find a video that will demonstrate it for you.

In the first book '**Budget Cooking for One – Supper Dishes**' I shared a lot of the recipes I have used myself over the years, recipes I shared with my children before they went away to University. For this book I have searched out and tried recipes from all sorts of different sources; friends, family, magazines, the internet etc. I have only included the recipes that were a success in my kitchen and adapt well to the 'budget' and 'cooking for one' labels.

I hope you enjoy trying them as much as I enjoyed the research and testing – I love that bit!

I included a few photos to give you an idea of what some of the dishes looked like when I prepared them in my own kitchen.

I have tried, where possible, to use American weights and measures (please forgive me if I get some wrong – I'm British...) but have included a simple conversion chart at the end of the book for European readers.

Another point to be aware of if you are not in America is that a couple of the branded ingredients listed may be difficult to source in your country, so improvise and experiment – I did. To be honest I had to 'Google' *Seasoning Vegetables* and *Velveeta* as I had no idea what they were.

I would encourage you to be creative and add extras to the recipes. You may have vegetables that need using up so add them to your dish. Add different herbs and spices to see what tastes good to you. Have fun cooking!

I hope this 'Budget Cooking for One – Book Two' cook book helps you to create interesting, cheap and mouthwatering meals that you will enjoy eating.

Store Cupboard Essentials

Please note: The following section on Store Cupboard Essentials is included in Book One of the Budget Cooking for One series. I have added a few extras that I feel are useful store cupboard items.

Your store cupboard will, over time, come to contain many of the ingredients you will need to try a new recipe.

Make it a habit to buy one item to add to your store cupboard each time you go to the supermarket. That way it won't cost a fortune but you will quickly build up a stash of staple ingredients for lots of recipes. Another thing I do is to grow some herbs in a window box on the kitchen windowsill. I grow chives, parsley, coriander (cilantro) and oregano at the moment and intend to grow more. It's really easy – even for a house plant killer such as myself...

Below is a list of things that I routinely have in my store cupboard but you may have other ingredients that you want to add.

Seasonings

Sea Salt
Black pepper
White pepper
Dried Herbs – your own preferences
Dried Spices – your own preferences

Dried Chili Flakes
Mustard Powder
Tomato Puree
Stock Cubes

Cans

Tomatoes
Tuna
Sweetcorn
Peanut Butter
Coconut Milk
Beans – baked beans, butter beans, kidney beans, black beans etc.

Bottles

Honey
Vinegar
Red or (and) White Wine Vinegar
Vegetable oil
Olive Oil
Extra Virgin Olive Oil
Vegetable Oil
Tomato Ketchup
Maple Syrup
Soy Sauce
Worcestershire Sauce
Mustard
Chopped Garlic

Dry Stuff

Flour
Cornstarch (cornflour)
Pasta
Oats
Rice
Noodles
Stock Cubes
Dried Mushrooms

Fridge

Crème Fraiche
Eggs
Milk
Cheese

Freezer

Vegetables – Peas, Green Beans, Sweetcorn etc.
Fruit – Raspberries, Strawberries, Gooseberries,
Rhubarb, Blueberries etc.
Bread – Part baked rolls and sliced shop bought
bread, Flour Tortillas etc.

Don't underestimate the usefulness of your
freezer. These days frozen vegetables are just as
nutritious as fresh ones as the manufacturers
freezing process has become faster. Bread can be
taken and used one or two slices at a time. You
may also want to freeze any leftover soups and

recipes you have made and divided to save for another day.

Another useful addition to your store cupboard is foil containers to freeze any extra portions of recipes you have left over for another day.

It is so easy to get stuck in a rut and make the same few meals over and over. So try and vary your meals by compiling a weekly menu, make a list of the ingredients you will need and do your shopping at the beginning of each week.

You will begin to look forward to mealtimes when you know that you will be having something different, nutritious, quick and simple to make and exactly to your own taste.

The following pages contain a selection of tried and tested dishes that are easy to prepare, most are economical and all are very tasty. An added bonus is that many of them are easily adaptable so you can add your own favorite ingredients.

Remember, variety is the spice of life and you should make sure that there is lots of variety in your diet.

Lime Grilled Chicken with Spanish Rice

This dish has the fabulous flavors of grilled chicken breast spiced with lime, and garlic, alongside the spicy flavor of long-grain rice, tomatoes and veggies.

Ingredients

1 boneless, skinless chicken fillet (butterfly it if it is really thick)
Sprinkle each of garlic powder, salt and pepper.
A sprinkle of bottled lime juice (or a squeeze of fresh...)
For the Rice:
1 cup water or chicken stock
½ cup long grain rice
¼ cup canned diced tomatoes with green chili
¼ cup frozen Seasoning Vegetables
Salt and pepper to taste

Method

Start by preparing the rice.

Add water or chicken stock to a large pan and bring to a boil. Add the rice, tomatoes, and vegetables and cover. Lower the heat and simmer for around 20 minutes, or until all the water has been absorbed. If the rice is still not done, add a little more liquid and continue cooking. Be careful not to burn the bottom of the rice.

While the rice is cooking, heat your grill or skillet over medium heat. Sprinkle the chicken breast with salt and pepper, and lime juice, and place it juiced-side down in the skillet, or on the grill. Sprinkle salt, pepper, and lime on the top of the breast. Grill the breast for about 3 minute per side. Don't over-cook it or it will dry out. Remove from the grill and let it rest for around 3-5 minutes before serving.

Serve the chicken on top of the rice and garnish with a spoonful of salsa or mayonnaise and a wedge of lime.

For a substantial meal you could serve with tostada chips and refried beans.

Crispy Herby Chicken with Potato Wedges

Ingredients

2 chicken thighs or 1 breast with skin on
1 potato
Extra-virgin olive oil as needed
½ tablespoon chopped fresh rosemary
1 teaspoon chopped fresh oregano
½ teaspoon garlic powder
Salt and pepper to taste

Method

Preheat the oven to 375F (190C).

Cut the potato into wedges and cook for 3 minutes in salted water. Drain and leave to cool.

Place chicken and cooled potatoes into a baking dish.

Mix rosemary, oregano, garlic powder, salt and pepper together in a bowl. At this stage you could add any other herbs or spices you want to try like chili flakes to give the dish a little kick. Add oil until you achieve a thin paste. Pour over chicken and potatoes and shake the baking dish to coat well.

Cover with foil and bake for around 25-35 minutes (or until cooked through) in the preheated oven. Remove the foil and return to the oven uncovered for the last 5 minutes. Baste regularly for extra crispness.

Serve immediately with green vegetables.

Spicy Salmon with Caramelized Onions

Although the ingredient list looks long, it is mainly seasonings for the salmon fillet. You can try any mix of your preferred herbs and spices for the rub. The fun of these type of dishes is the experimentation!

Ingredients

1 salmon fillet
1 – 2 tablespoons minced onion
½ teaspoon ground black pepper
½ teaspoon paprika
1 teaspoon balsamic vinegar
¼ teaspoon cayenne pepper
1 teaspoon minced garlic
1 teaspoon Dijon mustard
1 teaspoon brown sugar
½ teaspoon onion powder
¼ teaspoon salt
1 tablespoon olive oil

Method

Combine the black pepper, paprika, cayenne pepper, minced garlic, Dijon mustard, brown sugar, onion powder, and salt in a small bowl. Stir in ½ tablespoon of olive oil to make a paste. Spread the paste all over the salmon fillets, and set aside to marinate at room temperature for around 30 - 45 minutes.

Heat the remaining olive oil in a small pan over medium heat. Stir in the onion, and cook until tender and golden brown, about 10 minutes, stir in the balsamic vinegar. Heat a separate non-stick skillet over medium-high heat.

Cook the salmon fillets in the hot skillet until golden brown on each side, and no longer translucent in the center, about 4 minutes per side. Pour the browned onions and olive oil over the salmon fillets and serve with new potatoes and vegetables.

Chicken Quesadilla

Few things make a more outstanding lunch than a Quesadilla. They are easy and quick to make and the ingredients are interchangeable. For example, you could use shrimp, prawns or thin strips of beef or pork instead of chicken.

Ingredients

1 skinless chicken breast
½ cup grated cheese
1 large flour tortilla
1 scallion, chopped
(optional)
1 medium jalapeño
pepper (optional)
1 tablespoon butter, oil, margarine or you could even use white wine if you like
Lettuce, tomato, basil etc. for serving

Method

The secret to good quesadillas is not to cook them with the skillet too hot. Flour tortilla scorch easily.

Chop and cook the scallion and jalapeño pepper in oil for a few minutes until just beginning to soften. Put onto kitchen paper to drain.

Slice the chicken into strips and cook in a little butter, oil or wine until cooked through (around 5 minutes).

Spray a large iron skillet with non-stick spray (very lightly) and heat over a medium to low heat. When the skillet is hot, lay the tortilla in and scatter the cheese evenly over the tortilla. Next, sprinkle the onions, peppers, (if used) and cooked chicken down the center of the tortilla.

Cook until the cheese is melted. Slide onto a serving plate and let it cool for 2 minutes before adding lettuce, tomato, basil and any other salad ingredient you fancy.

Fold the bottom up and fold each side to the middle and serve immediately.

Onion Pan Fried Pork Chops

This dish is quick and easy to make and delicious with potatoes and vegetables on a cold miserable day.

Ingredients

1 or 2 pork chops
1 (1 ounce) envelope dry onion soup mix
¼ cup all-purpose flour
Olive oil or coconut oil for frying

Method

Before opening the onion soup mix, use your hands to crush the larger bits of onion in the packet. Open the packet, and pour the mix into a shallow bowl. Stir in the flour.

Heat the oil in a heavy skillet over medium heat. The oil is hot enough when a pinch of the flour mixture sizzles when tossed into the oil.

Coat pork chops in the onion soup mixture, and shake off the excess. Carefully place in the hot oil.

Turn chops over after about 30 seconds to quickly sear both sides. Cook for about 3 minutes per side depending on how you like your chops cooked. I like mine cooked so the coating is crisp and golden brown.

Serve with either a large crispy salad or especially good with mashed potatoes and lots of vegetables.

Marinated Grilled Fish Steaks

Ingredients

1 or 2 fillets of your preferred type of white fish
1 clove garlic, minced
3 tablespoons olive oil
1 teaspoon dried basil
1 teaspoon salt
1 teaspoon ground black pepper
1 tablespoon fresh lemon juice
Lemon zest
1 tablespoon chopped fresh parsley

Method

In a bowl mix together garlic, olive oil, basil, salt, pepper, lemon juice, lemon zest and parsley.

Place the fish in a shallow dish and pour over the marinade. Cover or seal and place in the refrigerator for at least 1 hour, turning the fish occasionally.

Preheat an outdoor grill for high heat and lightly oil grate. Set grate 4 inches from the heat. Of course you can cook them indoors but the flavor from an outdoor grill really adds to the dish.

Remove fish filets from marinade and drain off the excess. Grill filets for around 3 minutes per

side or until fish is cooked and can be easily
flaked with a fork.

Serve immediately with a large salad.

Eggplant Sandwich

A delicious sandwich for a
quick lunch or a TV snack.

Ingredients

1 small eggplant, halved and sliced
1 tablespoon olive oil, or as needed
¼ cup mayonnaise
2 cloves garlic, minced
2 (6 inch) French sandwich rolls
1 small tomato, sliced
½ cup crumbled feta cheese
¼ cup chopped fresh basil leaves

Method

Preheat your oven's broiler. Brush eggplant slices
with olive oil, and place them on a baking sheet
or broiling pan. Place the pan about 6 inches
from the heat source.

Cook under the broiler for 10 minutes, or until
tender and toasted.

Split the French rolls lengthwise, and toast. In a
cup or small bowl, stir together the mayonnaise
and garlic. Spread this mixture on the toasted
bread. Fill the rolls with eggplant slices, tomato,
feta cheese and basil leaves.

Top Budget Tip:

Save any leftover bread and turn into croutons or breadcrumbs. Cut stale bread into cubes and fry slowly in a little coconut oil and garlic until crispy. Put into container when cool and freeze. Whiz up stale bread in processor into fine breadcrumbs and freeze for later.

Macaroni Cheese

Another firm favorite for a
quick and delicious meal.

Ingredients

Short pasta for one, such as small shells,
orecchiette or macaroni
1 tablespoon butter
½ tablespoon flour
1 cup milk
Salt and pepper, to taste
1 teaspoon dry mustard powder
2 cups grated cheddar cheese or more depending
on how strong you like your cheese sauce
Handful grated parmesan for garnish (optional).

Method

Bring large pot of lightly salted water to a boil.
Cook the pasta until al dente.

Drain.

Meanwhile, add butter to saucepan over medium
heat. When butter melts, add flour and stir to
make a roux. Add the milk a little at a time
whisking well with each addition. Continue to
slowly add the milk until the sauce reaches your
preferred thickness.

Remove pan from heat. Stir in the grated cheddar. Taste and add more cheese if you like.

Add drained pasta. Stir to combine. Transfer to your serving dish.

Garnish with a sprinkle of grated parmesan cheese, chopped chives and dusting of paprika, if desired.

I like to pop mine into the oven for a few minutes to crisp up the top.

Serve with garlic bread.

Pork Schnitzel

I will assume for this recipe that you are making schnitzel for one meal. However, as I will be doing the breadcrumbs, egg and flour for a couple, I usually make extra to use up the mixtures as they freeze really well and don't take long to defrost for an easy meal.

Ingredients

1 or 2 pork steaks
½ cup all-purpose white flour
½ cup bread crumbs
1 egg
1 teaspoon paprika
½ tablespoon finely chopped chives
Salt and pepper to taste

Method

Bash the pork between 2 sheets of plastic wrap (cling film) with meat mallet or, if you don't have one, the bottom of a saucepan, until the meat is about ¼ inch thick.

Prepare a breading station by arranging 3 shallow bowls or pie plates with the following; flour seasoned with salt and pepper in the first, beaten egg in the second, and bread crumbs mixed with chives and paprika in the third.

Cover pork slices first in flour, dip in beaten egg and finally coat in the bread crumb mixture. At this stage you can freeze any you are not using immediately.

Heat a frying pan over medium heat. Add 1 tablespoon butter and ½ tablespoon olive oil. When oil is hot, add pork. Cook until golden brown on each side, about 1 to 2 minutes per side. Add a little more butter to the pan if it becomes too dry during cooking.

Remove schnitzel from pan. Transfer to paper towel to drain. Keep warm until ready to serve.

Goes really well with a few French fries and green veg or a large salad.

Parmesan Chicken Goujons

Children love these homemade chicken goujons (a 'goujon' is a small strip of fish or chicken, coated in breadcrumbs), they are the healthy alternative to the ones you can buy from the takeaway.

Ingredients

10 melba toasts or 1 cup stale bread
1 boneless, skinless chicken breast
1 egg
2 tablespoons grated Parmesan cheese
1 teaspoon dried oregano
salt and pepper
1 tablespoon vegetable oil

Method

Put melba toast (or any dry stale bread) in resealable plastic bag and close. Using bottom of a pot or rolling pin, bash until finely crushed.

Cut chicken lengthwise into strips about 1 inch thick.

Break egg into shallow dish; using fork, beat well. In another shallow dish, stir together melba toast (bread) crumbs, Parmesan cheese, oregano, salt and pepper.

Dip chicken strips into egg, letting excess drip off; dip in crumb mixture, turning to coat all sides.

Arrange on a greased baking sheet; drizzle with butter. Bake in preheated oven 425F (220C) until golden, crispy and no longer pink inside, about 10 -15 minutes.

Serve with a side of fries and salad and a small dish of garlic mayonnaise (or just simple mayonnaise if you prefer).

You could also use any type of firm fish instead of chicken for this recipe.

The Big Scrambled Egg Breakfast

Breakfast does not have to be boring. It is the most important meal of the entire day, and a hearty breakfast sets you up for the day. The 'Big Breakfast' will keep you going well into lunchtime.

Ingredients

2 eggs, beaten
2 pieces of toast
2 semi-thick slices of ham, cubed
¼ cup frozen Seasoning Vegetables (or, if you are tough and brave, fresh chopped onion and chopped jalapeño)
Knob of butter or margarine
Salt and pepper to taste
Cheese, mushrooms, diced tomatoes (optional)

Method

Put bread in the toaster or salamander (toaster-oven).

On medium heat, melt the butter in the egg pan. Add Seasoning Vegetables and sauté until they are translucent. Add ham and cook until lightly toasted. At this point, you can also add mushrooms, tomatoes, cooked, cubed sausage or anything else you fancy and heat through.

Check the toast. When it is done, remove, lightly butter, and set aside. Do not start cooking the eggs until the toast is almost done.

In a bowl, crack eggs, add 1 teaspoon water, and beat until the yolks and whites are evenly mixed. Add eggs to ham mixture and using a spatula, rake them to the center as they cook. Keep the eggs moving at all times, and if they start cooking too fast, remove the pan from the heat and continue stirring until you get control of them again. When the eggs are almost done, you can add cheese if you like. You just want the cheese to melt. Continue cooking until the eggs are done to your liking.

Arrange toast on a plate and spoon the egg mixture on top of each piece. Serve with lots of hot coffee and a glass of orange juice.

New England Fisherman's Platter

Like most New England food, this is simple, hearty, and delicious.

Ingredients

1 cup milk
1 fish fillet - any light fish like cod, trout, swai, tilapia, haddock, flounder, etc... Do not use tuna, salmon, shark or similar fish.
2 red potatoes, quartered and boiled (do not peel)
2 tablespoon butter or margarine
2 tablespoon flour
1 teaspoon salt, for the fish water
Salt and pepper to taste

Method

Spray 2 iron skillets with non-stick cooking spray.

In a large pot, add enough water to cover potatoes, a little salt, and bring to a boil. Add the potatoes.

While the potatoes are cooking, add 1 cup water and 1 teaspoon salt to one of the skillets and bring to a boil.

Add the fish fillet to the skillet with the boiling water. Allow fish to poach for around 4 minutes, gently turn it over and poach for another 2 minutes. Fish should be just starting to get flaky.

Carefully remove the fish to a plate. Reserve the water you cooked it in.

In the other skillet, melt the butter and whisk in the flour then whisk in the milk a little at a time. The roux will still be thick. Ladle in the water you cooked the fish in, one ladle at a time, whisking all the time, until you reach the thickness you desire. Add salt and pepper to taste.

Drain the potatoes and arrange them on the plate with the fish. Drizzle the sauce over both the fish and potatoes. For garnish, you can sprinkle a little dried parsley or chopped chives over the top.

Serve with a garden salad

Creamed Tuna (or tinned fish) On Toast

Another one of my favorites. It is so easy to prepare, and very filling.

Ingredients

½ cup milk or Evaporated Milk
1 small can of tuna (or tin of sardines, herring, or fish steaks)
½ tablespoon of flour
½ tablespoon of butter or margarine
Salt and pepper to taste.
2 slices of toast

Method

Arrange your toast on serving plate.

Spray a skillet with non-stick cooking spray. Melt the butter in the skillet over medium heat. Slowly whisk in the flour a little at a time, until you get a smooth roux.

Whisking all the time, add the half the tuna to the roux along with all the juice keeping the other half in chunks for later. The sauce will thicken rapidly, so be ready to add milk and continue whisking until you get a nice thick gravy-like texture. Adjust the milk as needed to get the right thickness. Remove from the heat and stir the remaining chunks of tuna through the sauce.

Add salt and pepper to taste, then drizzle the mix over the toast.

Top Budget Tip:

When cooking chicken, try boiling it in a large pot of water and a few vegetables. This keeps the chicken moist and succulent. When cooked, remove from pan and allow to cool. Strip the meat from the carcass and use for sandwiches and a dinner of chicken, potatoes and vegetables. Then make a hearty soup with any leftover bits.

The water used to cook the chicken can be frozen for a delicious home-made stock.

Pork Tenderloin with Mustard Sauce

A succulent pork tenderloin in a spicy, creamy mustard sauce - how much better could it get?

Ingredients

Pork tenderloin steak – whatever size you prefer
½ cup chicken broth
¼ cup cream
½ tablespoon Horseradish
½ tablespoon Dijon Mustard
1 knob of cold butter
1 teaspoon Cayenne or Red Pepper
1 teaspoon chopped chives
Oil for frying

Method

In a large sauté pan or iron skillet, heat 2 tablespoon of frying oil. Add the pork tenderloin, and brown it on all sides then cook to your liking.

When the tenderloin is cooked, remove it to a plate and let it rest. With a paper towel wipe the excess oil from the pan. Do not scrape the bottom.

Add chicken stock to the pan and bring to a boil. Stir it gently to get all the little bits of meat in the bottom of the pan to mix with the stock.

Add Cayenne pepper, horseradish, cream, and Dijon Mustard to the stock. Use a whisk to keep it well mixed, and smooth.

Simmer the sauce until it starts to thicken. Turn off the heat and whisk in a knob of cold butter. Stir in the chopped chives.

The tenderloin has rested long enough by now. Slice it and arrange on the plate.

Serve with roasted potatoes and a green salad.

Mediterranean-Style Baked Eggs

These are great for a light meal and really simple to make. The ingredient list is simply a suggestion and can be altered to your own preference.

Ingredients

2 eggs
1 tablespoon chopped olives, black or green, your choice
2 tablespoon diced tomatoes
2 tablespoon chopped fresh spinach
2 tablespoon feta cheese
1 tablespoon chopped basil
Salt and pepper

Method

Preheat the oven to 350^{0}F

In a mixing bowl, whisk all the ingredients together until evenly mixed.

Spray 2 compartments of a muffin tray, or 2 oven-proof ramekins with non-stick cooking spray

Pour the mixture in each of the two compartments (or ramekins). Bake for around 10 minutes or until set and golden brown.

Using a rubber spatula, ease the eggs out of their compartments to a plate.

Serve with a crisp green salad.

With this recipe you can add almost any ingredient you prefer.

For instance, if you don't like olives you could add a slice of cooked bacon chopped into small cubes. The vegetables can be exchanged for whatever you prefer.

Creamy White Wine Chicken

This baked chicken breast sits on a bed of leeks and covered with a creamy white wine sauce – delicious.

Ingredients

1 clove garlic
1 tablespoon chopped parsley
1 tablespoon olive oil
1 small leek
1 teaspoon cornstarch
2 tablespoons white wine
1 tablespoon crème fraiche or cream
4 tablespoons cold water
Salt and pepper

Method

Preheat the oven to 425F.

Mix minced garlic, parsley and 2 teaspoons of the oil in a small bowl.

Cut around 4 slits along the top of the chicken breast then rub the herb mixture all over especially over the cuts to make sure the mixture flavors the meat.

Spread the sliced leek loosely over the base of a small ovenproof dish – not too big or the sauce will burn. Add the remaining oil and toss the leeks to coat.

Place the chicken on top, season and bake for around 10 minutes. While the chicken is cooking, mix the cornstarch and wine until smooth and whisk in the crème fraiche (or cream) and water.

Take the chicken out of the oven and pour the sauce over. Return to the oven for 10 – 15 minutes or until the chicken is cooked through.

Transfer the chicken to a serving plate and stir the leeks and cream sauce then pour over chicken.

This dish is really nice with some wild rice.

Quick and Easy Spaghetti Carbonara

I love this recipe, it's really simple to make and tastes delicious.

Ingredients

2 oz. spaghetti, uncooked
1 garlic clove, minced
1 strip bacon
1 egg, slightly beaten
1 tablespoon cream
1 tablespoon chopped chives
Handful of Parmesan cheese, grated

Method

Place the bacon in a medium pan and fry until crisp. Transfer to a paper towel to drain.

Place the minced garlic in the same pan and cook in the bacon fat for 30-40 seconds, until aromatic.

Place the pasta in a pot of lightly salted boiling water and cook according to pack method. Drain in a colander and return to the pot saving a little of the pasta water.

Break up the bacon and add to the pot along with bacon fat and garlic. Add the beaten egg and cook over medium heat for 2-3 minutes. Keep stirring while cooking otherwise the egg will scramble. To loosen up the sauce add a little of the pasta water. Remove from heat and stir in the cream.

Put onto serving plate and sprinkle with parmesan cheese and chopped chives.

Season to taste, serve immediately.

Note: If you have some leftover cooked chicken you could add that to the carbonara for an extra meaty meal. Add the chicken when you cook the garlic to warm through.

Chicken Pilaf with Vegetables

With this recipe you can use the frozen vegetables as in the ingredient list or, if you have left over vegetables in the fridge – use those. As with a lot of the recipes in this book, you can use any vegetables you prefer, you don't have to stick to the recipe.

Ingredients

½ tablespoon sunflower oil
1 small onion, chopped
2 teaspoons curry paste
1/3 cup basmati rice
2/3 cup chicken broth
1 cup frozen mixed vegetables
½ cup baby leaf spinach, frozen or fresh (if using fresh you will need double the amount)
1 large or 2 small boneless, skinless chicken thigh fillets
Salt and pepper to taste

Method

Add the oil to a medium skillet and set over medium heat. Add the onion and cook for 5 minutes until soft and translucent.

Cut the chicken into cubes, add to skillet and brown for 3 - 4 minutes. Then add the rice and curry paste, give a stir and cook for a minute.

Pour in the chicken broth. Once the mixture begins to boil, slow down the heat to low, put the lid on the skillet and cook about 10 minutes.

Add vegetables, stir and let cook until the rice has softened and all the liquid is absorbed.

Season with salt and pepper to taste, stir and serve.

Cauliflower "Rice" Stir-Fry

Ingredients

1 cup cauliflower florets
1 tablespoon coconut oil
½ sliced red onion
2 minced cloves garlic
3 tablespoons vegetable stock
½ tablespoon fresh ginger minced
½ small red chili, thinly sliced
1 cup broccoli florets
1 medium carrot, cut into thin strips
½ red bell pepper, stemmed, seeded and diced (optional)
Juice of ¼ lemon
Salt and pepper

Garnish (optional)
1 tablespoon shelled pumpkin seeds
1 tablespoon fresh cilantro leaves

Method

Place the cauliflower in a food processor and process until it is finely chopped. Add ½ tablespoon coconut oil to a large griddle and set over medium heat. Add ¼ sliced red onion and 1 minced clove garlic and sauté about 4-5 minutes until softened. Stir in the cauliflower and season to taste.

Pour in the vegetable stock, cover with a lid and let cook until all the liquid has evaporated and the cauliflower becomes soft, 5-7 minutes. Remove from the pan and keep covered to stay warm.

In the same pan, heat 1 tablespoon oil over medium heat. Add the remaining red onion and sauté, stirring frequently, until it is golden and translucent. Stir in the remaining garlic, chili and ginger. Cook for 1 minute. Add the bell pepper, carrot and broccoli florets, and sauté stirring frequently until vegetables have softened, 5 minutes. Add the lemon juice, season with salt and turn off the heat.

Place the cauliflower "rice" into a serving plate and top with the roasted vegetables.

Garnish with cilantro and pumpkin seeds. Serve immediately.

Simple Prawn Korma

When making this mild curry I always make it for two servings. In my opinion curry tastes fabulous the day after you cook it. I have listed the ingredients I use for two servings. If you prefer making one serving, simply halve the ingredients.

Ingredients

1 medium onion
1 – 2 tablespoons mild curry paste
¼ pint cold water
3 tablespoons natural yoghurt
2 tablespoons mango chutney
2 tablespoons heavy cream
Large handful cooked and peeled prawns
Salt and pepper
Chopped cilantro for garnish
Boiled rice to serve

Method

Put the onion and curry paste in food processor and blitz. Keep lifting the lid and pushing the onion and curry paste down into the food processor to get a smooth paste.

Transfer the spiced smooth onion paste into a skillet and cook on a medium heat until the onions begin to soften. Add 2 tablespoons of the cold water and cook for a few minutes until the onions are totally soft.

Pour over the rest of the water, add yoghurt and mango chutney. Bring to a gentle simmer and cook until the sauce is thickened, stirring all the time.

Add prawns and cream and continue cooking until the prawns are heated through.

Put your cooked rice in a serving dish and spoon your delicious curry over the top.

Garnish with cilantro.

Chicken Soup with Pasta and Couscous

This is a delicious and satisfying soup that is low fat and anyone can prepare.

Ingredients

1 boneless skinless chicken fillet
1 cup water
8 oz. Vegetable or Tomato Juice
6 oz. frozen Italian Blend vegetables
1/8 cup small pasta shells
1/8 cup couscous
1 tsp Italian Seasoning
1 tsp garlic powder (or minced garlic)
Salt and pepper to taste

Method

Boil the chicken fillet in water until done. Remove the fillet and set aside.

Add all the rest of the ingredients to the water you boiled the chicken in (which is now chicken stock), and set heat to simmer. Cover and simmer for 15 minutes.

Shred or chop the chicken and add to the pot. Simmer for a further 5 minutes. Check that the pasta shells are cooked.

Of course you can add anything you fancy to this

soup – leftover vegetables (if cooked add with the chicken), different seasoning, chicken stock instead of tomato juice etc.

Serve piping hot with chunks of buttered crusty bread.

Top Budget Tip:

Peel and freeze any over-ripe bananas to add to a smoothie or simply whizz up in a processor for a fast banana ice cream.

Eggs in Bacon Baskets

These little breakfast treats are as delicious as they are impressive and simple to make. They would also make a great lunch served with a crisp salad.

Ingredients

4 slices of bacon
2 eggs
¼ cup ricotta cheese
Finely chopped parsley (or any herb you prefer)
Chopped chives for garnish
Salt and pepper to taste

Method

Preheat the oven to 350^0F

I use ceramic oven-proof ramekins for this, but if you don't have any, you can use 2 compartments of a muffin pan.

Line 2 ramekins (or muffin pan sections) completely with bacon slices. It works best if you weave the slices. Cut the bacon strips in half if needed to completely cover the bottom and sides of the ramekins.

In a measuring cup, break the eggs, add the cheese, salt, pepper, and parsley and whisk until

the mixture is evenly mixed. Pour the egg
mixture in the ramekins. Bake in the oven for 12-
15 minutes.

Using a rubber spatula, gently remove the
baskets from the ramekin and place on a plate.
Sprinkle finely chopped chives over whilst still hot

Serve with hot, buttered toast or, if for a lunch
dish, a tomato salad.

Note: For a spicy dish you could whisk a
teaspoon of chili powder into the egg mixture
before pouring into the ramekins.

Tuna Macaroni Casserole

This filling casserole is great for a cold winters night.

Ingredients

1 cup of cooked macaroni, cooled
1 small can of tuna, drained and flaked
4 oz. (¼ lb) Velveeta cheese
¼ cup of milk
1 thick slice of onion, diced.
1 tablespoon all-purpose flour
1 tablespoon butter
1 tsp. salt
½ cup grated cheddar cheese for topping

Method

Sauté the onion in the butter. Whisk in the flour and gradually add milk. Stir until the roux is smooth and thick.

Add the Velveeta and stir until it is melted.

Add macaroni, peas, tuna and salt. Mix well.

Spray a small oven-proof iron skillet, or small pan that is oven-safe with non-stick cooking spray

Pour the mixture into the pan, cover, and bake at 350 degrees for 30 minutes.

Remove the pan from the oven and set aside

Change the oven to Broil.

Scatter the grated cheese on top of the casserole, and place it under the broiler until the cheese is golden brown.

Garlic and Lemon Beef Tips with Rice

The secret to this dish is that the beef must be cooked very quickly, so that it doesn't have a chance to get tough. This is done all on high heat, and cooks in just 10 minutes. Not strictly a budget dish but I had to include it – it's delicious!

Ingredients

1 small sirloin steak, cut into strips
½ cup beef stock
½ cup white wine
½ cup All-Purpose Flour
1 tablespoon fresh chopped parsley
1 tablespoon olive oil
1 knob of butter
3 teaspoons chopped garlic
Juice and zest from ½ lemon
1 teaspoon Onion Powder
Salt and pepper to taste
1 cup cooked white rice (*preferably a long-grain variety...Basmati and Jasmine work well for this...*)

Method

Start the rice using your favorite method, mine is 1 measure rice to 2 measures water – fluffy rice every time!

Cut the sirloin into even sized strips. Add salt and pepper directly to the meat, then toss with the flour until well coated.

Heat olive oil in a non-stick skillet, over high heat. When oil is hot, add the steak, separating each individual strip so that all pieces will brown on all sides. When brown, add garlic and continue cooking for a few seconds. Add the butter. Stir constantly until the butter is melted.

Add the white wine. Continue cooking, stirring occasionally, until the liquid reduces by half. Add the beef stock and stir. Continue cooking until the liquid reduces by half. Add the lemon juice and the zest. Add onion powder, and salt and pepper to taste. Add the parsley. Simmer for just a few more minutes, then turn off the heat.

Your rice should be done by now. Serve beef tips over the rice, and enjoy!

Chicken and Grits

Based on the wildly popular Shrimp and Grits recipe, this is a wonderfully spicy, but relatively simple dish. It uses a simple 3-step cooking process. I have to confess that I haven't tried this as it's impossible to get grits in UK but an American friend told me I should include it.

Ingredients

For The Grits:
1 cup water
¼ cup yellow, or white grits
¼ cup milk, cream, or soy milk
1 oz Velveta, Sharp Cheddar, Queso Blanco, or regular cheese
One teaspoon butter or margarine
Pinch of salt

For The Chicken and Veggies
1 boneless, skinless chicken breast, grilled or pan-fried, and cubed
¼ cup frozen seasoning vegetables, or fresh combination of onions, celery and green peppers, diced
¼ cup canned diced tomatoes with green chilies
1 clove garlic, peeled and diced
1 fresh jalapeño pepper, seeded, deveined and diced
2 tablespoons olive oil
1 tablespoon butter or margarine

Salt and pepper to taste

Method

In a skillet or sauté pan, heat the olive oil over medium heat, and cook the chicken breast in it until done. Set aside to cool, then cut into ½ inch cubes. Set aside. Leave the olive oil in the pan.

Prepare grits by bringing the water to a boil, Add the milk and margarine. Add salt. Whisk in the grits, lower the heat and simmer until they are the consistency of creamy pudding. Lower the heat to low, add the Velveta, cover and allow it to melt. Stir well when it is melted. Keep grits warm.

In the skillet you fried the chicken in, over medium heat add the garlic, seasoning vegetables and jalapeños and sauté until the onions are translucent.

Add the tomatoes and chicken cubes, cover and simmer for 15 minutes. Add the butter to thicken the sauce slightly.

To serve, mound the grits in a bowl and ladle the chicken/veggie mixture over them, being sure to include the wonderful sauce.

Baked Fish in Foil

Ingredients

1 white fish fillet – whichever
fish you like best
½ tablespoon olive oil
1 fresh jalapeno pepper, chopped (optional)
1 teaspoon ground black pepper
2 teaspoons garlic salt
1 lemon, sliced

Method

Preheat oven to 400 F (200 degrees C). Wash the
fish in the cold water, and pat dry.

Brush the fillet with olive oil, and then sprinkle
with black pepper and garlic salt.

Take a large sheet of aluminum foil and place the
fillet in the center of it. Place the jalapeno slices
on the top, followed by the lemon slices.

Now fold the foil edges over until it resembles an
enclosed packet.

Lay the packet onto a baking dish and bake in the
oven for 10-15 minutes or until the fish flakes
easily with a fork.

Serve with buttered new potatoes and green
vegetables.

Note: If you are omitting the jalapeno pepper, you could add a bunch of fresh herbs to add flavor. Fish goes well with basil, chives, marjoram, parsley etc. Experiment with different flavors until you find your favorite.

Grilled Pitta Pizza

This pizza ingredient list is just a suggestion. You can have some real fun with this and use up any leftover vegetables and meat from the refrigerator or invent your own toppings.

Ingredients

1 teaspoon olive oil
1 pitta bread round
3 tablespoons pizza sauce (you could use tomato puree or tomato ketchup)
½ cup mozzarella cheese, grated
¼ cup crimini mushrooms (or any type of mushroom you prefer), sliced
Pinch garlic salt

Method

Preheat grill to medium-high heat.

Brush one side of the pitta bread with olive oil and then cover with pizza sauce.

Top with mushrooms and sprinkle with grated mozzarella. Season with garlic salt.

Coat the grill grate with oil and place the pitta pizza onto it.

Grill the pizza, covered, for about 5 minutes or until the cheese is melted and just turning golden.

Spicy Chicken

Ingredients

1 boneless skinless chicken breast
1 tablespoon nonfat plain yogurt
1 teaspoon garlic powder
½ teaspoon smoked paprika
1 tablespoon breadcrumbs
½ tablespoon Parmesan cheese
½ teaspoon basil
Salt and pepper

Method

Preheat oven to 350°F.

In a shallow bowl mix together the cheese, basil, breadcrumbs, salt and pepper.

In another dish mix together salt, pepper, garlic powder and smoked paprika.

Coat all sides of the chicken breast with a non-fat yogurt. Then season with salt, pepper, paprika and garlic powder mix.

Next, toss the chicken in the cheese mixture until evenly coated on both sides. Gently shake off excess.

Coat a skillet with cooking spray and set over medium-high heat. Add the chicken and cook for

3-4 minutes per side until it acquires golden crust.

Then transfer it to a baking dish lined with foil and bake in the oven for around 10 minutes or until cooked through, turning once.

Lovely with lemon couscous or even a few French fries.

Cilantro and Cumin Rubbed Pork Chops

Ingredients

1 pork chop
½ teaspoon salt
½ tablespoon ground cumin
½ tablespoon ground cilantro (coriander)
1 clove garlic, minced
2 tablespoons olive oil
Ground black pepper to taste

Method

Put the salt, cumin, cilantro and garlic in a bowl and mix with enough olive oil to form a paste.

Season the pork chop with salt and pepper, and rub with the paste.

Heat the remaining olive oil in a skillet over medium heat, and cook the pork chop about 5 minutes on each side or until cooked to your liking. Serve with grilled asparagus, grilled cherry tomatoes and a few basil or mint leaves.

Top Budget Tip:

Don't buy ready prepared and washed vegetables. Remember people wouldn't chop cabbage or peel carrots if there wasn't money to be made – your money.

So always buy the whole vegetable and wash, chop and prepare your own; it won't take long and you are saving money.

Herb-Rubbed Salmon Steak and Vegetables

Ingredients

Olive oil
1 salmon steak
2 tablespoons fresh mint, finely chopped
½ teaspoon dried oregano
½ teaspoon dried basil
¼ teaspoon smoked paprika
1 small garlic clove, minced
4 cherry tomatoes
1 scallion, thinly sliced
1 small zucchini, halved lengthwise, then sliced crosswise ¼ inch thick
Salt and ground pepper

Method

Preheat oven to 425 F (200 C). Put the salmon into a baking dish and coat with a little olive oil.

To make the rub, combine the oregano, basil, garlic, mint, smoked paprika, ¼ tsp salt, and a few turns of freshly ground pepper in a small bowl or pestle and mortar and combine thoroughly.

Coat all sides of the salmon with ½ of the rub and bake in the oven for 5-8 minutes or until it is opaque throughout.

While the fish is cooking, start frying the vegetables. Add a little olive oil to a frying pan and heat over medium heat. Add the zucchini and sauté stir frequently until soft, 7-8 minutes.

Add the tomatoes, scallion, and remaining rub mixture, stir and cook for another minute, until heated through. Season the vegetables with salt and pepper.

Place the cooked salmon onto a serving plate and serve with the herb vegetables and a few hot buttered new potatoes.

Scallion Rice with Shrimp and Soy-Lime Sauce

Ingredients

3 teaspoons vegetable oil
2 scallions, white and green parts separated, thinly sliced
¼ cup long-grain white rice
1 tablespoon fresh lime juice
2 tablespoons soy sauce
1 teaspoon sliced jalapeño or serrano chili
Coarse salt and ground pepper
¼ lb large shrimp, peeled and de-veined
2 tablespoon fresh coriander (cilantro)

Method

Add 1 teaspoon oil to a small saucepan and set over moderate heat. Stir in the scallion whites, season with salt and pepper, and sauté until they become tender, 2-3 minutes.

Next add rice, sauté for 20-30 seconds, then pour in 1/3 cup of water. When it begins to bubble, slow down the heat and let simmer, covered, until all liquid is absorbed and the rice has softened, around 10 - 12 minutes. Remove the pan from the heat and let stand 5 minutes.

Meanwhile, take a small bowl to mix together the lime juice, soy sauce and chili.

Add 2 teaspoons of oil to a small pan and set over medium-high heat. Toss in the shrimp and let cook 2 -3 minutes or until opaque throughout.

Using a fork, fluff the rice and sprinkle with chopped coriander and scallion greens.

Place the shrimp onto a serving plate along with cooked scallion rice and serve with the soy, lime and chili sauce mixture.

Pasta with Cheese and Mixed Greens

Ingredients

1 cup dried orecchiette pasta
2 cups mixed salad greens
2 tablespoons sun-dried tomatoes, chopped
1 tablespoon goat cheese, crumbled
2 tablespoons Parmesan, grated, plus more for garnish
Pinch salt
Pinch freshly ground black pepper
1 tablespoon olive oil

Method

Place the pasta in a pot of salted boiling water and cook over high heat until al dente, about 7-8 minutes.

Transfer to a colander to drain, reserving half a cup of the cooking water.

Place the salad greens along with sun-dried tomatoes, goat cheese and Parmesan in a medium salad bowl. Toss in the cooked pasta, pour in the warm half cup of pasta cooking water that you saved. Season the dish with salt and pepper to taste, drizzle with olive oil and mix to combine.

Sprinkle with grated Parmesan, if desired, and enjoy.

Spicy Chicken Stir-Fry with Peanuts

Ingredients

1 teaspoon peanut oil
1 clove garlic, thinly sliced
1 boneless, skinless chicken breast.
½ Serrano pepper, thinly sliced
1½ cups snow peas stem ends trimmed
Salt and ground pepper
1 tablespoon peanuts, toasted, chopped
1 tablespoon fresh lime juice
¼ cup basil leaves, chopped

Method

Add the peanut oil to a griddle and set over medium-high heat.

Thinly slice the chicken and sauté until brown on the bottom side, about 3 minutes. Turn the chicken and stir in the snow peas, chili, garlic, and 2 tablespoons water; and continue cooking until the chicken is cooked through, about 3-5 minutes.

Add the peanuts, lime juice, season with salt and pepper and stir to mix flavors.

Garnish with chopped basil and serve.

Note: I like to add a good handful of beansprouts as the snow peas to add a little extra bulk. You could also add some noodles instead. Be imaginative and add any extras that you fancy.

Cajun Pork Pasta

Ingredients

1 large pork steak
2 oz. linguine pasta
1 teaspoon Cajun seasoning
1 tablespoon butter
½ red bell pepper, sliced
½ green bell pepper, sliced
2 fresh mushrooms, sliced
½ green onion, chopped
1/6 cup grated Parmesan cheese
½ cup heavy cream
Pinch dried basil
Pinch lemon pepper
Pinch salt
Pinch garlic powder
Pinch ground black pepper

Method

Place the pasta in a pot of lightly salted boiling water and cook for 7-8 minutes until al dente. Transfer to a colander to drain.

Melt the butter in a large non-stick skillet over medium heat. Coat the pork evenly with Cajun seasoning and cook in the skillet for 4-5 minutes, until golden and cooked through.

Stir in the green bell pepper, red bell pepper, green onion and mushrooms. Cook for another 2 minutes.

Turn down the heat and stir in the cream. Add the lemon pepper, black pepper, basil, salt and garlic powder. Add the cooked pasta and stir to coat.

Cook for 2 minutes until heated through.

Sprinkle the grated Parmesan over the pasta mixture and serve with garlic bread.

Fried Potatoes for One

Ingredients

1 tablespoon butter
2 small potatoes
½ tsp season salt
¼ tsp onion powder
¼ cup cheese, grated
¼ tsp garlic powder
½ tablespoon bacon bits

Method

Peel the potatoes and place in a microwave safe bowl. Let cook in the microwave for about 3 minutes, until fork tender.

Transfer to a cutting board and when cool enough to handle, chop the potatoes into small cubes.

Place the butter in a skillet and set over medium heat.

Add the potatoes and fry until crispy and golden. Season with salt, onion and garlic powder.

Sprinkle the potatoes with cheddar cheese followed by bacon bits. Turn off the heat and leave to stand for at least 2 minutes until the cheese melts.

Delicious served with any of the fish dishes in this book. I particularly like these potatoes with the Herb Rubbed Salmon Steaks.

Note: If you like spicy food you could add chili powder along with the onion and garlic powders. Experiment with different spices to find your favorite.

Oyster Stew

Apparently this is a New
England Classic with the rich
taste of oysters and the
creamy sweetness of milk. Again, this is a recipe
sent to me by my American friend.

Ingredients

2 cups milk or Evaporated milk
1 can of oysters (not smoked and do not drain)
2 tablespoon butter
Salt and pepper to taste

Method

Empty the oysters, juice and all, into a saucepan.

Now, here is the secret: Using the open-side of
the can, with a slight twisting motion, chop the
oysters into small pieces. I've tried doing it other
ways, but it just isn't the same unless you use
the can it came out of......Weird, I know, but it's a
150 year-old tradition. Who am I to question it?

Put the sauce pan on the stove on Med-Hi heat.
Add the butter and allow it to melt, then simmer.
Simmer the oysters for about 2 minutes.

Add the milk. Salt and pepper to taste. When the milk is hot (almost boiling) remove from heat and serve.

Chicken or Pork Piccata

This is one of my favorite ways to prepare chicken fillets or pork steaks.

Ingredients

1 boneless, skinless chicken breast fillet or pork steak
1 cup of flour (for dredging)
1 tablespoons butter or margarine
About 1 tablespoon chicken stock or water (could be more or less)
2 tablespoons olive oil
2 teaspoons capers
Salt and pepper to taste

Method

Place a skillet (frying pan) on the stove on a medium heat. Add half the butter and half the olive oil.

While the oil is heating, salt and pepper your meat on both sides and dredge it in the flour. If the meat is very thick, bash it out with a rolling pin to make it a uniform thickness so it cooks evenly.

When the oil is hot, gently add the meat. Cook for around 3 minutes, or until the bottom is golden brown. Flip it over and cook until the other side is golden brown. Remove the meat to a plate to rest.

Add the rest of the butter and olive oil to the pan. Put 2 teaspoons of the dredging flour in the oil and stir until it is smooth. Cook out for about a minute.

Add the chicken stock (or water) and stir until the desired thickness is reached.

Adjust water/stock as needed. Add the capers, then the meat back to the pan. Simmer for around 1 minute, flip the meat, and simmer for another minute.

Remove meat from pan, to a serving plate. Pour sauce over the meat.

Serve with vegetables, potatoes or rice.

Speedy Chicken Chili

I don't know about you but I think any chili
tastes so much better the day after. So I usually
make this, leave it in the refrigerator overnight. I
reheat thoroughly and have it for dinner the next
day with warm naan bread – delicious! For me
this recipe makes two meals so I freeze some in
a foil container but that all depends on your
appetite.

Ingredients

1 boneless skinless chicken breast (or any fish or
meat you prefer)
½ tablespoon vegetable oil
1 small onion, chopped
1 chopped sweet green pepper
1 teaspoon chili powder
1 teaspoon dried oregano
½ teaspoon salt
¼ teaspoon pepper
½ can diced tomatoes
½ can black beans or kidney beans, drained and
rinsed
¼ cup corn kernels

Method

Trim any fat from chicken breast; cut into small
even sized cubes. In large heavy saucepan, heat
oil over medium-high heat; cook chicken for

about 2 minutes each side or until no longer pink inside. Transfer to plate.

Add onion, green pepper, chili powder, oregano, salt and pepper to pan; cook over medium heat stirring often, for about 5 minutes or until vegetables are softened.

Add corn, tomatoes and beans. Turn up the heat and boil stirring all the time, for 5 around minutes. Put the cooked chicken (or whatever cooked meat or fish you are using) into the sauce and continue to simmer for a further 2 or 3 minutes.

Serve over rice or on its own with chunks of garlic bread.

Sticky Orange Chicken

Ingredients

Olive oil, as needed
1 medium sized potato, cut into wedges
1 red onion, cut into 4 to 6 wedges
3 garlic cloves, skin on, ends removed or smashed
Salt and freshly ground pepper
1 whole chicken leg
1 or 2 tablespoons honey (or more, your choice)
1 tablespoon apple cider vinegar
1 small rosemary sprig
½ teaspoon dried rosemary
1 seedless orange, cut into wedges
½ tablespoon orange zest, for finishing

Method

Preheat oven to 400 degrees F. Drizzle 1 tablespoon of olive oil in a baking dish.

Add potatoes, onions, garlic cloves and salt and pepper to oil in the baking dish. Toss to combine. Set aside.

Cut chicken leg in half to separate the thigh and the drumstick.

In a large bowl add salt and pepper, honey, apple cider vinegar, rosemary and dried rosemary. Stir well to combine. Add chicken pieces and orange wedges and stir gently into the sauce making sure the chicken is well coated. Tip the whole lot into a baking dish.

Cover and bake until chicken is cooked through and potatoes are tender, turning occasionally, about 35 - 45 minutes. For an even stickier chicken, drizzle with 1 to 2 tablespoons more honey before serving.

Top with freshly grated orange zest and serve either with a crisp green salad or lots of broccoli.

Shrimp Lemon Pepper Linguini

Ingredients

Handful fresh shrimp, peeled and deveined
Linguine pasta for one
1 tablespoon olive oil
3 cloves garlic, minced
½ cup chicken broth
¼ cup white wine
Juice of 1 lemon
½ teaspoon lemon zest
Salt to taste
2 teaspoons freshly ground black pepper
¼ cup butter
3 tablespoons chopped fresh parsley
1 tablespoon chopped fresh basil

Method

Bring a large pot of lightly salted water to a boil. Add linguine, and cook for 9 to 13 minutes or until al dente; drain.

Heat oil in a large saucepan over medium heat, and sauté garlic for about 1 minute. Mix in chicken broth, wine, lemon juice, lemon zest, salt, and pepper. Reduce heat, and simmer until liquid is reduced by about half.

Mix shrimp, butter, parsley, and basil into the saucepan. Cook for 2 - 3 minutes, until shrimp is opaque. Stir in the cooked linguine, and continue cooking for around 2 minutes, until well coated.

Chicken with Rice and Bean Broth

Ingredients

1 Chicken Leg
1 - 2 tablespoons olive oil
1 small onion or shallot
½ cup uncooked long grain rice
1 cup water or chicken broth
½ cup drained black beans
½ cup corn kernels
Salt and pepper to taste
Your choice of spices for the rub

Method

Put your chosen spices (i.e. cumin, smoked paprika, chili powder etc.) into a dish with salt and pepper and mix well. Rub the mix all over the chicken leg.

In a pot over a medium heat sauté the chicken leg in 1 tablespoon of olive oil until it is golden brown on both sides. Remove chicken from pot and set aside.

Add remaining oil to pot and add chopped onion. Cook for about 2 - 3 minutes then add the rice stirring all the time. Continue stirring over medium heat for another minute then add the liquid, beans and corn kernels. Bring to a simmer then put the chicken back in the pot.

Turn the heat down to low and cover with a tightly fitting lid. Cook for a further 25 -30 minutes turning the chicken once.

The dish is ready when the rice is cooked and the chicken juices run clear when cut into.

You may need to add more water or broth if the rice is not cooked to your liking.

Asian Noodles with Bacon

Ingredients

2 slices smoked bacon
2 scallions
½ cup frozen peas
½ chopped mushrooms
Grated carrot
1 teaspoon cornstarch
1 cup vegetable stock
¼ teaspoon paprika
½ teaspoon Worcestershire sauce
One portion cooked noodles – either dried or fresh

Method

Cut the bacon into 1 inch pieces then fry. Add the finely chopped white part of the scallions, peas, mushrooms, carrot and paprika and cook until vegetables are tender.

Mix the cornstarch with a little of the stock to form a thin paste and stir into pan. Add the rest of the stock, noodles and Worcestershire sauce.

Simmer for a few minutes until sauce has thickened then scatter with the chopped green parts of the scallion.

Top Budget Tip: Using up left-over puff pastry.

If you have any ready-made puff pastry left over you could make some cheese twists and cook in same oven as your Mini Savory Pies.

You will need:

Left Over Puff Pastry, grated Gruyere cheese, good pinch smoked paprika and some beaten egg.

Mix the paprika into the cheese and sprinkle evenly over the rolled out left-over puff pastry. Fold the pastry in half and roll a little to seal the cheese into the middle. Cut into ½ wide strips and gently twist.

Place on baking tray and brush with beaten egg. Bake until crisp.

Store in airtight container.

Hearty and Creamy Tomato Soup

This delicious soup recipe produces 3 or 4 portions so you can freeze some for another day or works great for a packed lunch in a vacuum flask.

Ingredients

1 tablespoon butter
½ red onion
1 leek
1 clove garlic
1 peeled potato
1 carrot
1 cup vegetable stock
1lb ripe tomatoes, deseeded and chopped
1 tablespoon tomato puree
½ cup full fat milk
Seasoning to taste

Method

Finely chop onion, leek and garlic. Grate the carrot and potato.

Melt the butter in a large saucepan over a low heat and cook the onion, leek and garlic until soft but not browned. Add the carrot and potato and cook for 5 minutes.

Add the stock and bring to simmering point then add the tomatoes and tomato puree then season with salt and pepper. Simmer for around 10 minutes until the vegetables are really soft.

Add the milk and warm through then liquidize the soup with a stick blender.

I would usually pass the soup through a sieve as I like a smooth consistency, but you decide how you like yours.

Heat well before serving.

Note: If you don't have any ripe tomatoes you can substitute these for canned plum tomatoes.

Barbeque Chicken

Delicious served hot or cold so these are another good addition to a packed lunch.

Ingredients

2 chicken drumsticks without skin
1 shallot
1 garlic clove, minced
1 tablespoon tomato puree
¼ pint water
2 tablespoons red wine vinegar
1 tablespoon Worcestershire sauce
1 tablespoon mustard

Method

Finely chop the shallot and place in bowl. Add minced garlic, tomato puree, water, vinegar, mustard and Worcestershire sauce. Whisk until well blended.

Rinse the chicken and pat dry with kitchen paper. Place the chicken in an ovenproof dish and pour over the sauce. Leave to stand for at least 2 hours occasionally spooning the sauce over the chicken.

Preheat the oven to 375F. Cook the chicken in the oven for 20 – 25 minutes or until the juices run clear when a skewer is inserted into the thickest part of the meat.

During cooking spoon the sauce over the chicken a few times to keep moist.

Serve immediately with a salad or a few French fries or leave to cool and chill in the refrigerator until ready to eat.

Mini Savory Pies

These little pies are
simple to make and
freeze well so it's worth
making 6 so you can save
some for another day.

Ingredients

Knob of butter for greasing
Ready-made puff pastry
Flour for dusting
3 eggs
½ cup milk
1 cup grated mature cheddar cheese
1 slice ham, chopped into small pieces
1 sliced tomato
Seasoning to taste

Method

Preheat oven to 400F and grease a deep 6 hole
muffin tin or you could use the individual sized
flan tins (as used in the picture).

Roll out the pastry on a floured board until really
thin. Cut out 6 rounds to fit the size of the muffin
hole, making sure that the pastry extends just
above the rim of the hole.

Whisk the eggs and milk together in a bowl, add
salt and pepper. Divide the cheese between the

pastry cases, add pieces of ham to each then pour the egg mixture over the top.

Top each with a tomato slice.

Bake in a preheated oven for around 20 minutes or until risen and golden brown. Remove from oven and leave to cool a little before removing from muffin tin.

Spaghetti with Lamb Meatballs

Ingredients

1 tablespoon breadcrumbs
½lb minced lamb
2 clove garlic minced
1 egg
½ tablespoon parmesan cheese
1 tablespoon olive oil
2 teaspoon dried rosemary
1 can chopped tomatoes
½ tablespoon tomato puree
1 teaspoon sugar
Spaghetti for one
Salt and pepper

Method

Place the breadcrumbs, minced lamb, 1 clove garlic, egg, cheese and seasoning into a large bowl. Mix well until all the ingredients are combined.

Form the mixture into small balls – wet your hands with cold water to keep the mixture from sticking to your hands. Place the meatballs into the fridge for about 30 minutes.

Heat the oil in a saucepan and add the other clove of garlic and dried rosemary. Stir for 1 minute. Add the can of tomatoes, tomato puree and sugar and bring to the boil then reduce the heat and simmer for 5 minutes. Carefully place the meatballs in the pan and spoon the sauce over them. Cover and simmer for around 15 minutes, turning the meatballs occasionally.

Meanwhile cook the spaghetti according to the package instruction.

Drain and place in warm serving bowl. Top with the meatballs and sauce and a little grated parmesan cheese. Serve with garlic bread.

Chili Cheese Baked Sandwich

Ingredients

2 slices thick bread, buttered
6oz grated cheese
2oz softened butter
1 fresh chili or 1 teaspoon chili flakes
½ teaspoon ground cumin

Method

Preheat the oven to 375F.

Mix cheese and butter in a bowl until well combined, then mix in the chili and cumin.

Place one slice of bread, buttered side down, on a baking sheet then spread the cheese mixture on. Place the other slice of bread on top, buttered side up and press down.

Bake in the preheated oven for 8 – 10 minutes or until crisp and golden brown.

Serve immediately. Lovely with a crisp salad or a spicy salsa.

Chorizo and Cheese Quesadillas

Ingredients

2 flour tortillas
½ cup mozzarella cheese
½ cup cheddar cheese
4oz chorizo sausage, diced
2 scallions, finely chopped
1 chili, deseeded and finely chopped
Vegetable oil

Method

Place all the ingredients together in a bowl and mix thoroughly. Season with salt and pepper.

Place the mixture on one of the tortillas then top with the other tortilla.

Brush a large frying pan with oil and heat over a medium heat. Add the quesadilla and press it down with a spatula, cook for 3 – 4 minutes until the bottom is crisp and lightly browned. Turn the quesadilla over and cook the other side until the cheese has melted.

Cut the quesadilla into quarters and serve.

Fast Falafel

Ingredients

1 onion
1 clove garlic
1 tablespoon fresh parsley
1 teaspoon ground cumin
1 teaspoon ground coriander
½ teaspoon baking powder
Salt and cayenne pepper
1 can chickpeas
Oil for frying

Method

Drain the chickpeas, place in food processor and blend to a coarse paste. Chop the onion and crush the garlic then add to the processor. Add the rest of the ingredients and blend again to mix thoroughly.

Cover and leave to rest for 30 minutes, then shape into small balls. Leave to rest for a further 30 minutes. Heat the oil in a large saucepan or deep fat fryer until a cube of bread browns in 30 seconds. Very carefully drop in the balls and cook until golden brown

Remove from oil and drain on kitchen paper. Serve hot with hummus, crisp lettuce and tomatoes.

Some Simple Conversion Figures

IMPERIAL TO METRIC

1 oz = 30g
4 oz = 110g
1lb   = 450g

1 fl.oz = 30ml
5 fl.oz or ¼ pt = 150ml
20 fl.oz or 1pt = 600ml

OVEN TEMPERATURES

130C = 110C fan = 250F = Gas mark 1
150C = 130C fan = 300F = Gas mark 2
170C = 150C fan = 325F = Gas mark 3
180C = 160C fan = 350F = Gas mark 4
190C = 170C fan = 375F = Gas mark 5
200C = 180C fan = 400F = Gas mark 6
220C = 200C fan = 425F = Gas mark 7
230C = 210C fan = 450F = Gas mark 8
240C = 220C fan = 475F = Gas mark 9

AMERICAN SPOON MEASURES

1 level tablespoon flour = 15g flour
1 heaped tablespoon flour = 28g flour
1 level tablespoon sugar = 28g sugar
1 level tablespoon butter = 15g butter

AMERICAN LIQUID MEASURES

1 cup US = 240ml
1 pint US = 480ml
1 quart US = 950ml

AMERICAN SOLID MEASURES

1 cup flour = 125g flour
1 cup butter = 225g butter
1 cup brown sugar = 170g brown sugar
1 cup granulated sugar = 170g granulated sugar
1 cup icing sugar = 100g icing sugar
1 cup uncooked rice = 170g rice
1 cup chopped nuts = 100g chopped nuts
1 cup fresh breadcrumbs = 150g fresh
breadcrumbs
1 cup sultanas = 140g sultanas

Thank You

Thank you for buying this book and I really hope it has given you some inspiration for simple, economical and interesting meals to prepare for yourself. Remember, most of these recipes can be adapted to your own personal taste by adding your own favorite ingredients. So be adventurous and change things around a bit – this is how family favorite recipes are actually born!

If you enjoyed this second book in the series 'Budget Cooking for One' I would really appreciate it if you would leave a review on Amazon. *Simply type in the title and author in the search bar of Amazon, click on the book and leave your review.* Thank you so much.

If you are interested in receiving notification of the next book in the 'Budget Cooking for One' series, *please leave your email address* at the address below.

www.eepurl.com/SZOLH or scan the QR code to go straight to the signup page

If you have any simple recipes for one that you would like to contribute to my next book, please email me.

Penelope.Oates21@gmail.com

Upcoming Books in the 'Budget Cooking for One' series:
Slow Cooker Cooking for One
Simple Single Serving Desserts
TV Snacks for One
Chicken Recipes for One
Delicious Salads for One

Thank you again.

Penny

Your Notes

Your Notes

Made in the USA
Middletown, DE
03 May 2018